"*Create the* **HIGHEST, GRANDEST VISION** possible for your life because you become WHAT YOU BELIEVE."

—Oprah

"*Most of the reason* we don't do things is because we're **afraid to fail**. I just made a decision one day that I was not going to do things in MY LIFE BECAUSE OF FEAR."

—Sara Blakely

A Mindset Journal to
Help You Rise in Leadership
& Rock Your Sales Results

SAY
Yes!
THEN FIGURE IT OUT

JENNIFER DARLING

Table of Contents

Introduction

I spent March 2020 to June 2021 being a couch potato. Although my virtual business was booming, I was working long hours at my computer, constantly on Zoom, and barely standing up for more than a few minutes a day.

Then, my birthday rolled around in June 2021, and with it came a countdown: only two months until I would be on the road for my first in-person keynote presentation in eighteen months. I was overweight and out of shape. I had no idea how I was going to stand for two back-to-back in-person presentations, each to thousands of audience members. Still, I knew I held a coveted position at the BMW Supplier Diversity Conference, and it was critical that I show up and deliver an amazing speech—to present myself as a leader in the speaking industry, for women business owners, and for my client.

There was no time to wait. I had to act. I drove to the gym, signed a year-long contract, and hired a personal trainer. On my first trip to the gym, even fifteen minutes on the "granny bike" was pushing it. It would've been easier to give up, but I kept that keynote—and all my leadership and business goals— in mind, and I progressed each day until I was bored of that bike and needed something else.

Of course, the journey to showing up as the leader you want to be is never a straight line, and soon I had a setback. The month after my birthday—one month before the conference—I took a trip to Michigan to see my niece. She invited me to a cardio drumming class, and I accepted the invite. On the day of the class, however, I backed out. I returned home upset with myself for not going.

So I went back to Michigan to make it right. This time I stuck to my commitment and went to the class with her. And do you know what? It was *so much fun*! It was challenging. And sweaty. And there was a lot of heavy breathing. And I loved it!

When I came back home, I spent hours online looking for a cardio drumming place near me, with no luck. A few months prior, that would've been the end of the story. I would've given up. Now, however, along with my physical health, my mindset had begun to change, and I was determined to keep this amazing new self-care and exercise routine in my life.

"Fine," I thought. "I'll just do it myself. I'll become a cardio drumming instructor." I said *yes*, committed to figuring it out.

In the meantime, it was time to turn all my energy toward the keynote. I had worked with my personal trainer to increase my stamina and was physically prepared to deliver my talks. With that physical and mental energy, I rocked them both! The audience feedback was stellar, and I walked away from the keynote on cloud nine with a renewed dedication to speak on more stages.

When I got home, though, I hadn't forgotten my commitment to myself. In September, I found an online cardio drumming training program and, with the help of an amazing mentor who encouraged me and pushed me beyond my comfort zone, I was certified as a Pound Pro instructor. Within six months, I had taught my first class at the YMCA.

I had just said "yes" to doing something very important to me. Something that will bring me years of joy, happiness, and fulfillment. Something that challenges me beyond my comfort zone. Something that makes me feel great and gives that feeling to others as well.

If you had told me on my birthday in June that I'd be teaching an exercise class by the end of the year, I never would have believed you. But when I said *yes* to something calling me, I realized I had everything I needed to figure out how to make it happen.

Why open a business-centric book with such a personal story? Because saying *yes* to myself in my personal life has affected my business in so many ways.

- I have a more positive attitude, which boosts my team's energy as much as mine.
- I have far more clarity when working with my clients.

- My resilience has increased tenfold, allowing me to speak to more audiences and spread my sparkle to the world.
- My business finances have catapulted.
- My entire way of being has shifted.
- Saying *yes* to cardio drumming has upleveled my leadership in every aspect of my life.

And that's what this guided journal is about. Not cardio drumming, per se (though I'd be happy to talk to you about that anytime, anywhere), but about developing a mindset that allows you to say *yes* to what you need and who you are—at home and at work.

Jennifer

SAY *Yes* in Life and Business

As leaders in business—as C-suite executives and aspiring leaders, coaches, consultants, entrepreneurs, and business professionals—there is no end to what we can achieve when we learn to say *yes* to the opportunities that come our way.

However, saying *yes* isn't always easy.

I've worked with women in business for over twenty years, and too often I've seen outstanding female leaders hesitate to step fully into their light. I've watched as they played small, holding themselves back and not taking full advantage of the roles they play in their organizations—with their teams, industry peers, their communities, the media, their customers, and even themselves.

Based on my experience, the number-one obstacle holding these amazing women leaders back is fear. Fear of rejection, of failure, of seeming egotistical, of not being good enough…you name it, we're taught, one way or another, to fear it. As a result, our inner voices are constantly shouting all the reasons we *can't* do something. Every time we take a step toward a new challenge, the alarms go off again, sometimes so loudly that we get scared and step back into our comfort zones. One step forward, then one step back. We call it being "stuck."

The trouble with being stuck is that we aren't just keeping ourselves small—we are also holding other women leaders back. By not stepping up and stepping out, we deprive our fellow ladies of other women to follow. When we learn to say *yes* to what we're called toward—even if it's a "longshot," even if we have no idea how to achieve it—if we learn to say *yes* and then figure it out, then we can obliterate that glass ceiling both for ourselves and for the women working alongside and coming behind us.

That's why I created this journal. To give you the tools and the confidence you need to develop a *Yes!* mindset—the kind that empowers you to say *yes*, make a commitment, and then figure out the details.

There's never been a more exciting time to be a woman business leader. The world of business has changed forever, and we have the responsibility to shape the future the way we know it needs to be. The business community needs us. Our industries need us. I'm tired of seeing rosters of leaders and speakers with few, if any, female faces. The communities we live in need us. We know a thing or ten about how to spin all the plates required to manage work and home and family all at once. We need to own that—for ourselves and for other women who need us to lead the way so they can step into their own greatness. It's about time for us to show others what it means to live a life where we can have it all—a successful career, a happy family, and a healthy body. We get to take all the old-school ideas that worked for us and combine them with new ways of living and doing business to take us to heights that may have been unimaginable before. It starts with learning to say *yes*.

We get to set new rules, decide how we want to show up, determine who we want to grow with, and establish balance that brings us joy, fulfillment, and happiness. We can do all of this while also paving the way for our future female leaders.

Now is the time to say *yes* to what is calling you!

How to Use This Book

*A*re you ready to say *yes* and then figure it out? Then, you're in the right place. *Say Yes! Then Figure It Out* is a guided journal that will help you develop the *Yes!* mindset you need to rise in leadership, making the changes in your personal life and business that will free you up to meet and exceed even your most outlandish goals.

There are eight sections in this guided journal. Each includes a personal story or two, some practical insights, and a list of journal prompts to help you think through and plan out your own journey to a *Yes!* mindset. We'll start with a self-evaluation to support you in identifying where your mindset is currently helping you and where it might be holding you back, then we'll work through each of the keys to cultivating that positive, growth mindset. You'll learn strategies and tips to:

- Let go of obstacles you can't control—and find ways to control what you can.

- Address negative triggers in a positive way.

- Identify and live your core leadership values.

- Create an environment that empowers you to say *yes!*

- Commit firmly to what you want.

- Allow your *Yes!* mindset to spread to those around you.

- Nurture your *Yes!* mindset continuously—even when things get hard.®My ultimate goal with *Say Yes! Then Figure It Out* is to help you develop and embrace the positive, *Yes!* mindset you need to show up in your professional life as the leader you want to be. Along the way, I'll ask you to do plenty of reflecting and work on your personal life, too, because **mindset isn't something we just grab on the way out the door in the morning and then hang up in the closet when we get home from work**. Our mindsets carry us through every part of our lives, impacting how we show up for ourselves and relate to others at home, among friends, and at work. To be an authentic leader, to have integrity in your professional life, you've got to put in the work at home, too.

With that in mind, I encourage you to give yourself plenty of time and space to really reflect on the journal prompts in each section. Don't try to jot down your answers in five minutes between meetings; instead, treat yourself to several hours to focus on yourself. You deserve it! You can answer every prompt in order, skip around to what calls to you and challenges you, or let the provided prompts inspire other, related reflections. This is your journey.

I've provided the roadmap, but detours are always welcome.

I've included space within this book for you to respond to the journal prompts, but feel free to add extra paper or supplement with your favorite notebook as needed. Use your most colorful pens, doodle inspirational comics in the margins, paste in inspiring images…this is your journal, and I want it to become a source of inspiration, joy, and confidence.

Ready to Get Started?

Before you go any further, think of two big ideas you haven't said *yes* to yet. Make one personal and one professional. Write them down here and keep them in the back of your mind as you work through the ideas and prompts in this journal. By the time you're finished, my hope for you is that you're ready to say *yes* and then figure it out.

Your Mindset, Before And After

If you don't know where you've come from, you don't know where you're going.

-Maya Angelou

The best way to chart the course toward where you want to go is to really understand where you are now. Then, you can start to identify your strengths and development opportunities, planning to leverage what you're already doing well and improve in the places where you might be holding yourself back.

Early in my sales career, I really didn't think much about mindset and attitude. I certainly didn't make it a priority to evaluate, analyze, or even consider how my mindset affected my business or any other areas in my life. Little did I know how much doing so would change my entire life.

There was a point in my corporate career where I was extremely unhappy, depressed, and anxious. I often felt hopeless, and at times, I even suffered from panic attacks. I recall going into a boardroom for a meeting one day. Even though it was 115 degrees where I lived, I was in a wool coat because I couldn't shake the chills. Then, as soon as I drove home, my ailments would dissipate. To an outsider, my life looked perfect: perfect job, excellent income, great marriage, beautiful home, and fancy car. However, on the inside, I was a hot mess. I couldn't live this way anymore.

At the time, I had a book on my shelf from one of my favorite sales mentors, Jeffrey Gitomer. It was called the *Little Gold Book of Yes! Attitude*. I loved Gitomer's work—I'd read all his books— but I'd always glossed over part of this one, and I wondered if it could inspire me now. I opened right to Gitomer's "Attitude Self-Assessment" and, with a pencil in hand, I began to look at different areas of my life that affected my attitude. What I discovered was that much of what was happening was actually within my control. I could *do* something about it.

When I read this book, I realized the importance of mindset in sales and every other area of my life. I also learned that my attitude sucked. For the most part, I was a positive person with a positive outlook on life, but there were things I was unaware of that were keeping me from my full potential. No wonder I was always feeling stressed, overwhelmed, and unfulfilled in my jobs and in life. No matter how much money I made, or how many awards I won or promotions I earned, I was unhappy. I was letting my inner critic and external environment control my thinking.

Mindset was everything, and yet I had put no attention toward mine. I decided to change that. I started by focusing on two or three areas, as Gitomer had suggested, and after I was feeling good about my improvement in each area, I would find the next area to focus on.

Since then, I have focused on my mindset nearly every day, choosing to think positive thoughts and surround myself with people and strategies that help me get there. Do negative thoughts frequently find their way into my brain? All the time. But the more I practice a positive mindset, the quicker I can shift my focus and the more courageous I become.

I hope you'll take the next step in your mindset journey by assessing where you are now so you know exactly where to focus your time and energy to make the biggest improvements. That's what this chapter is all about.

- First, spend a few moments with these ten prompts, reflecting on your current mindset and how it might be affecting your life in undesirable ways.

- Next, use my mindset evaluation (inspired by Gitomer's but rewritten based on my own research, observations, and experience) for a deeper understanding of where you are and what your journey toward a positive mindset might look like.

- Finally, use the prompts at the end of the chapter to reflect on what you've learned about where you are and where you want to be.

YOUR MINDSET NOW

1. What is your first response to trying something new?

_____

_____

_____

_____

_____

2. When you experience change, what does your inner critic say to you?

_____

_____

_____

_____

_____

_____

_____

3. What positive words would you use to describe your mindset?

_____

_____

_____

_____

_____

_____

_____

_____

4. What do you appreciate about your current mindset? What would you like to change?

_____

_____

_____

_____

_____

_____

_____

5. In your experience, how does your mindset affect your business?

_____

_____

_____

_____

_____

_____

_____

_____

6. How does your mindset affect other aspects of your life?

_____

_____

_____

_____

_____

_____

_____

_____

7. Is your attitude stopping you from reaching your full potential? In what ways?

_____

_____

_____

_____

_____

_____

_____

8. Reflect on a time when your mindset held you back from achieving a goal or showing up the way you wanted to. What happened? Why do you think you got stuck?

_____

_____

_____

_____

_____

_____

_____

9. In what ways do you think your mindset contributes to your success in life and business?

_____

_____

_____

_____

_____

_____

_____

_____

10. In what ways do you think your mindset contributes to the success of others around you?

_____

_____

_____

_____

_____

_____

_____

_____

_____

_____

_____

_____

_____

_____

_____

_____

_____

_____

_____

_____

_____

_____

_____

_____

_____

_____

_____

Mindset Self-Evaluation

Mindset Self-Evaluation: Part I

How to take this assessment: Enter the number that represents your current situation. Then add up your score for part one and put it on the line that says "Score Part 1." Do the same thing in part two, only notice the numbers are in reverse. Add the score for part two and put the total on the line that says "Score Part 2." Total both parts and refer to the scoring chart for your results.

1= All the Time 2= Often 3= Occasionally 4= Hardly Ever 5= Never

1. I am overwhelmed _____
2. I compare myself to others _____
3. I have a hard time letting go of things that bother me _____
4. I worry that I don't have enough money _____
5. I don't get enough sleep _____
6. I skip workouts _____
7. I eat unhealthy foods _____
8. I am hard on myself when something goes wrong _____
9. I work too much _____
10. I am always busy _____

Score Part 1: _____

Mindset Self-Evaluation: Part II

1= NEVER 2= HARDLY EVER 3= OCCASIONALLY
4= OFTEN 5= ALL THE TIME

1. I have a great work-life balance _____
2. I am enthusiastic about all areas of my life _____
3. I embrace change _____
4. I am flexible _____
5. I seek differing points of view _____
6. I surround myself with positive people _____
7. I celebrate my wins before I move on to the next thing _____
8. I plan time for self-care _____
9. I like how I am being _____
10. I have plenty of time to do the things I want _____
11. I am ready and willing to try new things _____
12. I take care of myself before others _____
13. I read or listen to books, podcasts, and trainings to expand my mindset _____
14. I have a wish list of things I want to do in my life and check it off frequently _____
15. I am willing to be fully transparent and vulnerable _____

16. I let others do things for me even when it's easier to do it myself _____

17. I challenge others to go outside their comfort zones _____

18. I give my team opportunities to step into their full potential _____

19. I am fully present when I'm with others _____

20. I acknowledge and embrace my unique qualities _____

21. I have a written list of my core values and refer to them weekly _____

22. I exercise regularly _____

23. I have a healthy relationship with food _____

24. I get ten to fifteen minutes of sunshine a day _____

25. I count my blessings every day _____

Score Part II: _____

TOTAL SCORE (add parts I and II): _____

Now use the chart on the next page to assess your mindset.

TOTAL 0-70: It's all good; you have a new awareness of what it takes to have a positive mindset. Choose one to three areas that you would like to put your attention toward improving. Write each idea on a sticky note and post them on your bathroom mirror or in your office. Work on these three things until you're satisfied, then pick the next area of focus.

TOTAL 71-100: You have several areas where you're demonstrating a positive mindset, but could things improve? Yes! Look for patterns in your high and low scores, identifying areas where you're already crushing it and areas where you could use a little extra work. Acknowledge yourself for the wins, then select one to three areas you would like to improve. Make a list and determine one action you could take toward improvement. You'll be on your way to more fulfillment in no time.

TOTAL 101-150: Welcome to the Big Club! This is where most people are. You think you have a *Yes!* mindset, but there's plenty of work left to do. The great news for you is that you have tons of momentum. Look at the list, identify one to three areas you would like to improve, and watch your joy and fulfillment soar!

TOTAL 151-175: Hey there, Rockstar! You should be teaching this stuff (maybe you are). You're doing great…keep up the good work and *crush it*! Use your experience and gifts to support others in their journeys to a positive mindset.

MINDSET GOALS

1. What did you learn from the mindset self-evaluation?

_____

_____

_____

_____

_____

_____

2. What are the top three areas in which you want to commit to improving over the next ninety days?

_____

_____

_____

_____

_____

_____

_____

3. What action steps will you take to improve in these areas? (You'll get more ideas as you work through the rest of this journal, but I find it inspiring to brainstorm right away!)

_____

_____

_____

_____

_____

_____

_____

4. What will you change about your life and your business by focusing on these areas?

_____

_____

_____

_____

_____

_____

5. Are there any other areas you might add, which are not in the assessment, that are important for you to take action on?

_____

_____

_____

_____

_____

_____

_____

_____

6. What is the ideal mindset you'd like to cultivate for yourself?

_____

_____

_____

_____

_____

_____

_____

7. What inspires you to do this work? Who and what (besides, of course, yourself) are you doing it for?

_____

_____

_____

_____

_____

_____

_____

8. Imagine being met with a challenging scenario once you've made progress in developing your ideal mindset. How would the "new you" handle that scenario?

_____

_____

_____

_____

_____

_____

_____

9. What are some things you've done recently that challenged your beliefs or assumptions about yourself?

_____

_____

_____

_____

_____

_____

_____

_____

10. What would happen if you stopped believing that you're limited by your abilities or circumstances?

_____

_____

_____

_____

_____

_____

_____

_____

SAY *Yes!* **THEN FIGURE IT OUT**

_____

_____

_____

_____

_____

_____

_____

_____

_____

_____

_____

_____

_____

_____

_____

_____

_____

_____

_____

_____

Let Go of What You Can't Control

Grant me the serenity to accept the things I cannot change, the courage to change the things I can, and the wisdom to know the difference.

—Serenity Prayer

*F*or many of us, the biggest drags on our mindset are the things we have no power over. That hardly seems fair! Well, here's the secret: those circumstances we can't control…they only control us *if we let them.* The first step to developing a positive mindset is to clear out the deadweight by letting go of all the things we can't control so we can focus our energy on the things we can.

In February 2020, I was three years into my business and was thrilled to have a calendar full of paid speaking engagements. I was ready to get on planes, fly across the world, meet new people, and get paid to do what I love. Within the next thirty days, it had all changed. I received call after call that my speaking engagements were canceled due to COVID, and I found myself lying in bed, depressed, for two solid weeks. Although I knew everyone in the world was having the same experience, that didn't make it any easier.

One day in March, I attended a Zoom call with my friend Jake Ballentine. He's a professional speaker and a dear friend who always has wise words at the exact moment I need to hear them. I remember Jake saying that, although we can't do anything to change the situation, the way we respond to it is fully within our control. We had all heard speculations that the pandemic would lead to a recession, but Jake's response floored me. He said he decided he was not going to participate in it.

I thought he was absolutely nuts! How could he not participate? After all, we had plenty of evidence— from news broadcasts to social media posts to empty grocery store shelves to my never-ending stream of client cancellations—that things were going to get much, much worse. What could I do when none of this was within my control?

Jake was adamant that we had a choice: We could let all those things we couldn't control stop us in our tracks, or we could rally behind the things we *could* control and find a way to thrive despite it all. I was skeptical, but what did I have to lose? I decided to say *yes*, joining Jake in his declaration that neither a pandemic nor a recession would stop us from working toward our goals.

Once I made that declaration, it was time to figure it out. I began by recalling other times in my life when things had appeared out of my control. Here are a couple big ones:

- **September 11, 2001**: I was working at a TV station, and in the wake of this tragic day, in our normally bustling department, you could hear a pin drop. The circumstances were far out of our control, and we were all tempted to curl up and hide, but we had a responsibility to report the news, so we reset our mindsets, picked up our chins, and led the way.

- **2006, just ahead of the Great Recession**: I had just accepted my first sales management position with a TV station when we lost 25 percent of our advertising revenue. We could've folded—after all, we didn't control the economy, so what could we do about it? But that's not what a success mindset looks like. Instead, we said *yes* to writing a new strategy, and we figured out how to do things differently than we had before. The result? Record-breaking years throughout the depths of the economic downturn.

So here I was again, left with a choice as the bottom dropped out: I could give up and crawl back into bed, or I could find a way to take control of the situation.

I chose to take control.

I knew people would be looking for virtual opportunities to learn how to keep their own businesses afloat, so I hosted a free online training to teach people how to use LinkedIn for business marketing. I launched it at the end of March with 250 students enrolled. Even though I gave the course away for free, I made offers within the training that helped me earn $10,000 in sales that month. It was clear to me that I was using something within my control to provide value for others—and work toward my own financial and leadership goals—so I kept going. Month after month, I kept offering free trainings and making more sales than I had the month before.

Even though the training was driving the sales, I quickly realized it wasn't really the free training that was the reason for my success. It was my decision not to be controlled by the things I couldn't control. It was my determination to take charge of what I could and to hold myself—not the global pandemic, not the recession—accountable for my success.

And, just like before, things turned out ok. In fact, they were better than ok! I went from zero dollars to over six figures in 2020, and it catapulted my business to multi-six figures after that. And all because, rather than wallowing in the circumstances outside of my control, I figured out what I *could* control, and I took back the reins.

Now, I want you to think about how you're letting factors that are outside of your control dictate your mindset and your success. They don't have to be as big as a global pandemic (though, of course, they can be!). They can be small distractions like an annoying coworker who talks too much or loud construction outside your office window. You can't change these things, but you do have a choice: You can let them kill your mood and your productivity, or you can change the way you respond (buy noise-canceling headphones or work from a coffee shop during the loudest parts of the day) and keep on moving.

3

CONTROLS

1. List five things outside of your control that you feel are holding you back.

_____

_____

_____

_____

_____

_____

2. List five things you *can* control.

_____

_____

_____

_____

_____

_____

3. Pick two of the things you wrote down that are holding you back, and brainstorm three choices you can make to overcome those circumstances.

_____

_____

_____

_____

_____

_____

_____

4. Pick two of the things you can control, and write out one action you can take toward controlling those things.

_____

_____

_____

_____

_____

_____

_____

5. Describe a time you let your external environment control your thinking. What could you have done instead?

_____

_____

_____

_____

_____

_____

_____

6. Describe a time when something big happened that was out of control, throwing you off course. How did you respond?

_____

_____

_____

_____

_____

_____

_____

7. Next time something like that happens, how will you like to respond differently?

_____

_____

_____

_____

_____

_____

_____

_____

8. What value can you provide to your audience, even when it feels like everything is out of your control?

_____

_____

_____

_____

_____

_____

_____

_____

SAY *Yes!* **THEN FIGURE IT OUT**

9. As a leader, what's the impact you have on your team when you act as if outside factors completely control your business?

_____

_____

_____

_____

_____

_____

_____

10. Conversely, what happens when you take control and find new ways to work?

_____

_____

_____

_____

_____

_____

_____

_____

_____

_____

_____

_____

_____

_____

_____

_____

_____

_____

_____

_____

_____

_____

_____

_____

_____

_____

_____

_____

Cultivate Positivity

*F*or years I have struggled to get this book started. I have struggled with being someone who talks about the importance of a positive attitude, because I'm not someone who has a positive mindset every day. I used to beat myself up for not immediately recognizing the "silver lining" in everything. I thought that, if I wanted to speak or write about positivity, I had to master it myself. Finally, I realized it was unrealistic to be positive all the time and that my definition of mastery should not be about perfection but about always working toward improvement in whatever area you're hoping to master. No matter how great at something you are, there's always room to go to the next level.

When I realized this, it became much easier to get this book started. Because in reality, this is not about having a positive mindset 100 percent of the time. This is about recognizing when we experience resistance, evaluating the situation, and making a decision about where we want to put our attention. There are always ways to say *yes* to what is most important.

Positive thinking sounds like such a simple concept, but for many of us, it's a full-time job! The good news is, if you struggle to make positivity your default, it's because you were built that way. Literally. Our brains are wired to receive negative messages. In a room full of hundreds of happy faces, we will immediately zero in on that one guy who's not smiling, because he's the one who poses a "threat," and our brains have evolved to identify threats so we can protect ourselves. Neuroscientists have identified a particular part of the brain, the amygdala, as the source of this alarm system, and scientists aren't the only ones interested in this phenomenon. Buddhists have been studying this pattern for centuries, and they call it "monkey mind." In psychology circles, you might hear it referred to as "negative bias" or your "inner critic." Whatever term you want to use, there's no doubt that we are more susceptible to negative messages than positive ones. It's a good thing we have this alarm system, because it protects us from harm. Unfortunately, though, it's a little hypersensitive to what really constitutes a threat, and it tends to go off whenever we're moving out of our comfort zones, which is where growth happens. Sure, leaving the comfort zone can *feel* like a threat, but it's almost always a positive move in the long run. If only our amygdala could understand that…

Too much negativity can affect our relationships, our performance, our happiness, and even our physical health. Even minor negative experiences can add up and take a toll on us. If we want to show up as our best selves—healthy, energetic, likable, and resilient—we have to start cultivating positivity. (To be clear, this doesn't mean putting on our rose-colored glasses and becoming a bunch of Pollyannas. Positivity isn't a replacement for realism or common sense, but it is a powerful companion to both, allowing us to see and work toward expansive potential instead of being blinded by limitations and obstacles.)

If you're skeptical of the power of positivity and positive thinking, you're not alone. But if you've seen it in action, you know what I'm talking about. I attended the Leukemia and Lymphoma Light the Night walk several years ago, and it was the most powerful demonstration of the effects of positive thinking I've ever seen. I was surrounded by thousands of people, all carrying lights and walking in support of this deadly blood cancer. Survivors carried red lights, those who'd lost loved ones honored them with white lights, and the many, many supporters carried yellow. The sky was dark except for the thousands of red, white, and yellow lights on the capitol lawn.

About halfway through the walk, a woman in a superwoman costume passed me. She was jumping and cheering and celebrating. "We can beat cancer!" she chanted. Then I noticed she was holding a red light. She had *already* beat cancer. I could tell by her electrifying personality that she was practicing a *Yes!* mindset, and there was no doubt in my mind that her positive outlook had helped her through her treatment.

How do we start cultivating positivity in our own lives?

Knowing what triggers you is the start to making positive changes in your life. A trigger can be anything that sets off a negative reaction in us. It could be something someone says, a situation we find ourselves in, or even just a thought that pops into our heads.

Here are a few common trigger possibilities:

- The internet is slow
- Drivers are going too fast or too slow
- The line is super long at Starbucks, and you're running late but tired as heck
- Your employee just called in sick on the day of a big proposal you needed them to present
- The weather
- News
- Rude or unreasonable people
- Not enough sleep or bad food
- Someone just took your parking spot

If we're not aware of our triggers, they can easily catch us off guard and send us into a downward spiral of negativity. But if we learn to identify our triggers, we can be prepared to deal with them in a more positive way.

One way to identify your own triggers is to pay attention to your thoughts and emotions throughout the day. When you notice yourself feeling down, getting irritated, or experiencing overwhelm, pause and try to identify what caused those feelings. Write the experience down in as much detail as you can. What just happened? What are you thinking? How are you feeling? How are you behaving? Why is this situation concerning you? Do you like how you are reacting? Do you like how you are being?

Once we've identified our triggers, there are a few steps we can take to actively cultivate positive thinking.

First, we can try to catch ourselves *before* we start reacting negatively. If we're aware of our triggers, we can be more mindful of our thoughts and actions in the moment.

Second, we can choose to respond to triggers in a positive way. This might mean taking a step back, giving yourself a five-minute time out to listen to music, taking a short walk to cool off, or snuggling with your pet. Once you've let your brain unwind, ask yourself how you can respond to the situation in a way that is in alignment with who you are.

Full transparency: my initial reaction to my triggers is not to take a step back but rather to scream, get ticked, be short with people, or get a raging headache. I'm still a work in progress, and I have to remind myself mastery is not perfection—mastery is being willing to see the situation from another point of view and taking action to improve. However, the more I practice a positive mindset, the quicker I notice my reactions and change my response. After I scream into a pillow, I'll walk outside, take a few deep breaths, and sit in the sunshine without my cell phone. I'll close my eyes and feel the sun on my face. After about five minutes, my head is clearer and I can decide how I want to move forward.

For very tough situations, I get out my list of core values (you'll determine your core values in the next section) and read them aloud. I ask myself who I want to be when responding to the situation. That always calms me down and allows me to proceed in the way I want to be in the world.

Finally, we can work on changing our mindsets. It takes time and effort, but it's worth it in the long run. We cannot avoid our triggers, but we can develop a greater awareness of them so we know what to do the next time we experience them.

Having a positive mindset is a choice—it's up to us whether we let negative experiences define us or whether we choose to focus on the good things in life. So next time you're feeling down, frustrated, overwhelmed, or ticked off, make the decision to cultivate positivity and see how it transforms your life for the better.

4

POSITIVITY

1. Many of us have been faced with the most difficult times in our lives beginning in March 2020. We can choose to focus on all the negative things that happened or look at it all another way. What good has come out of this challenging time? How have you grown as a person?

_____

_____

_____

_____

_____

2. List all the ways you can start practicing a positive attitude in your professional life.

_____

_____

_____

_____

_____

3. What are your most common negative triggers?

_____

_____

_____

_____

_____

_____

_____

_____

4. When you are triggered, what are some of your initial reactions?

_____

_____

_____

_____

_____

_____

_____

_____

5. Go back to page 24 and look at the list you made of ways your attitude is stopping you from reaching your full potential. Reframe those obstacles as assets.

_____

_____

_____

_____

_____

_____

_____

6. Describe a time when you allowed your inner critic to get in your way. What could you have told that voice instead?

_____

_____

_____

_____

_____

_____

_____

_____

7. What types of events tend to trigger your inner critic or your negative biases?

_____

_____

_____

_____

_____

_____

_____

_____

8. Think about a challenging situation you faced recently. What good came from it?

_____

_____

_____

_____

_____

_____

_____

9. Considering that same challenge, ask yourself, "How did I grow as a person through that challenge?"

_____

_____

_____

_____

_____

_____

_____

_____

10. Next time you're triggered, what can you do differently to have a more positive outcome for yourself?

_____

_____

_____

_____

_____

_____

Lead from Your Values

How Do You Want to Show Up in the Business World?

When my friend Amy told me she was nominated for an award in her industry, we celebrated. Then, she told me she didn't think she was going to accept the nomination. She didn't want public recognition, or to take all the credit, because she believed it was her team, not her, who should be recognized.

I hated hearing that. So I reminded Amy of several core leadership values she had previously shared with me, one of which was to be an inspirational leader. When I think back on my corporate career, I realize I was often the only female on the management team. I suspect it was the same in most companies. In fact, remember the audience members I mentioned in the introduction, who struggled to think of businesswomen they could look up to? The same was true for me when I was young in my career. When I think of female leaders I could look up to, the list was very small. I needed an Amy to look up to, and so do young leaders today—particularly young female leaders. If Amy was going to embrace that core value of inspiring others, accepting this nomination was a powerful opportunity to do so. Her other leadership values included supporting her employees in growing into their own leadership roles and being a mentor for women leaders in STEM. The way I saw it, Amy had a responsibility to accept this nomination—not for her own ego or recognition, but for her employees and all the other women CEOs, leaders, and emerging leaders in business— and especially in businesses dominated by men.

Well, wouldn't you know, Amy won! We encouraged her to post about it on LinkedIn, and again, her inner critic spoke up and she didn't want the spotlight on her. I reminded her what the award represented: her team, women running companies, and women in STEM. She wrote a post highlighting those people instead of herself, and it blew up with comments and celebrations. Amy was showing up in the business world as the type of leader she wanted to be and the type of leader people want to follow: authentic, heart-centered, caring, and courageous. These are some of the attributes of an influencer and thought leader. Yet, Amy wouldn't describe herself that way. She's humble, and she would rather honor others than be honored herself.

So, how do you want to show up in the world, in your business, or online? Whether you recognize it or not, you already have a reputation in every circle (these days, even *not* being online says something about you). Here's the good news: you can control that reputation, because you get to choose how you show up. If you don't, others will choose for you. You can be humble, and you can *also* be a thought leader, influencer, trusted advisor, mentor, trailblazer, changemaker, pioneer, and badass! You decide.

Core Values of Influential Leaders

Like Amy, you have a role to fill that is greater than you. If you look beyond your inner critic and consider your greater purpose, the gifts you were given to contribute to others, you'll see that you have been chosen to be an influential leader. Over the next few pages, I'm going to walk you through an exercise to help you identify your core values. If you need inspiration to get you started, feel free to peruse this word bank!

(L)EADERSHIP VALUES

• Courage	• Resilience	• Empathy
• Authenticity	• Integrity	• Humility
• Expansiveness	• Patience	• Respect
• Supportiveness	• Honesty	• Reliability
• Commitment	• Transparency	• Empowerment
• Vulnerability	• Generosity	• Passion
• Positivity	• Caring	• Curiosity
• Creativity	• Innovation	• Inspiration
• Responsibility	• Adaptability	• Strategy
• Authority	• Learning	• Consistency
• Teaching	• Responsiveness	• Open-Mindedness
		• Problem-Solving

Identify Your Core Values

Your core values are the qualities that are most important to you. It doesn't matter if you're in your office, on a plane, in a restaurant, or online—you represent these core values everywhere, and when your everyday life is anchored in these values, you can't help but embody the mindset that makes you the leader you want to be. Work through the following exercises to identify your own core values.

1. In the table below, write down the names of the five to seven people you admire in the left-hand column. Then, consider the qualities and attributes you admire about each person, and list them in the middle column. Save the third column for the next step!

PEOPLE I ADMIRE	QUALITIES I ADMIRE IN THESE PEOPLE	OTHER VALUES I ADMIRE

2. Circle any qualities and attributes that show up more than once. They're likely the core values that come naturally to you. After all, we often see the qualities in others that we have in ourselves. If there are any values that appear only once but really have energy for you, circle those, too. Then, if there are any other values that aren't on the list, write those down in the last column of the table.

3. On the next page, write down each of the values you circled and added. This list can be as long as you want. There is no limit to the number of values that are important to you. Once you've finished, tear that page out of the workbook and post it somewhere visible so you can refer to it daily.

These are my core values. I know they are mine
because they're the values I admire most in others.

_____'s Core Values

_____

_____

_____

_____

_____

_____

_____

_____

_____

_____

_____

_____

_____

_____

_____

5

VALUES

1. How was that process for you?

_____

_____

_____

_____

_____

_____

2. Did you identify any core values that surprised you?

_____

_____

_____

_____

_____

_____

_____

3. How do you think having this list will support you during a challenging situation?

_____

_____

_____

_____

_____

_____

_____

_____

4. In what ways do your core values affect how you show up as a leader in your industry?

_____

_____

_____

_____

_____

_____

_____

5. In what ways do your core values affect other areas of your life (business, relationships, health, financial, spiritual)?

_____

_____

_____

_____

_____

_____

_____

_____

6. How does this list of core values represent how you currently show up in your business?

_____

_____

_____

_____

_____

_____

_____

7. What values are important to you that are not currently showing up in your business, and what impact does that have?

_____

_____

_____

_____

_____

_____

_____

8. Choose up to three values you would like to focus on. What will you do to demonstrate these values in your business?

_____

_____

_____

_____

_____

_____

_____

9. What action will you take to get there?

_____

_____

_____

_____

_____

_____

_____

_____

10. In what ways does stepping into your values affect others around you?

_____

_____

_____

_____

_____

_____

_____

_____

Create a Yes! Environment

There are two types of factors that affect your mindset:

1. **Internal factors are your thoughts, beliefs, and attitude.**

2. **External factors** are things outside of you, in your environment, like the weather, other people, and the economy.

While we don't have total control over all these factors, we do have an opportunity to set ourselves up for success so that we can maintain a *Yes!* mindset when things seem to go haywire. One of the ways we can do that is by choosing a foundation that supports us to be at our best. This foundation is what I call creating a *Yes!* environment.

There are three key components to a *Yes!* environment: surrounding yourself with the right people, breaking the rules, and practicing self-care.

Let's look at some opportunities we have, as leaders, to create the kind of *Yes!* environment that will inspire us and support us in our growth journeys.

Surrounding Yourself with the Right People

1. Our Teams

Our support teams are the most powerful competitive advantage we have in our businesses and one of our most valuable assets. I've been managing teams for fifteen-plus years, and the single most important thing I've learned is to hire for the talent of the person and not the needs of the organization. If you do that, you will meet the needs of the organization. For example, when I need a person to assist me, I always start by learning about what they love to do and what they don't like to do. I give them assignments based on what they love to do and find someone else who loves to do what they don't. I've hired over a dozen people in the last five years, and all of those people are with me today. They are doing work they love and feel fully supported. When they feel that way, I don't have the stress of needing to have difficult conversations, and I feel fully supported, too.

Every year, I host a team retreat. We book a location outside our offices, have fancy meals together, and exercise together. (I love leading them in cardio drumming activities!) At the beginning of every retreat, we start with everyone sharing their goals for the year, unrelated to my business. These goals might be related to their work, but they can also be related to their personal lives. Then, I run a half-day personal development workshop for my team, because I want them to know just how important their goals are to me and that I will do what I can to support them.

We do not have a traditional hierarchy in my business. My team works *with* me, not *for* me. This is a big difference from my experience in my corporate job. I value my team and will do what I can to make sure they feel it.

I also recognize there's not a person on the planet who is perfect. When someone on my team makes a mistake, I remind them they are human, and we do make mistakes. I must let them know it's not worth beating themselves up; instead, I focus on what we can learn from it and ask them how they suggest we solve the problem. They always have solutions, and I can't recall a time where I didn't support their solution 100 percent.

Equally important to surrounding yourself with positive, talented people who share your values, unfortunately, is letting go of those who do not. One negative person can often take more of your energy and attention than all the positive people combined. There's just not enough time to allow that to happen when you are on a path of growth. This is also true for clients. Energy-draining clients are not worth the time we put into them. Typically, these are the ones who require far more than what they pay for and are never satisfied. If they suck your time and energy (your two most precious things), they are an expense, not revenue. We may find ourselves ruminating over frustrating situations with them when we could be focusing on supporting clients who make us feel awesome. Clients are a part of our team. We can choose to work with those who add value to our lives the same as we choose a support team to add value to our business.

2. Mentors, Advisors, Consultants, and Coaches

Where in the world would I be without the awesome mentors, advisors, consultants, and coaches in my life?

Regardless of the size of your business, you'll want to surround yourself with mentors, advisors, consultants, and coaches. And yes, all four are different! Here's a breakdown:

- **Mentors:** A mentor is a more experienced person who provides guidance and support to a less experienced individual. A mentor can help with things like career advice, personal development, and educational opportunities.

- **Advisors:** A professional advisor is someone who provides expert services in a particular area, such as financial planning, bookkeeping, and legal services. Advisors can be helpful for people who need experts to provide on-the-ground support or even handle certain responsibilities for them.

- **Consultants:** A consultant is someone who provides expert advice in a particular area, equipping you with the tools you need to do the work yourself. This can be helpful when trying to figure out things like how to start a business, how to market a product, or how to improve a process. You share your challenges, and they provide suggestions for solutions based on their expertise.

- **Coaches**: A coach is someone who helps people achieve their personal or professional goals. A coach can help with things like developing a plan, setting goals, and staying on track. They support you to find your own answers.

I always valued mentors, advisors and consultants, such as my leadership mentor, my accountant, my banker, my attorney, my personal trainer, and my sales consultant, but in my corporate job I had never even heard of having a coach (besides in sports). I had no idea what an important team member I was missing in my business.

When I started my speaking business, I enrolled in the National Speakers Association's Speakers Academy to learn how to run a business as a professional speaker. During my training, I met a business coach named Caterina Rando. The first time I met her, I knew I had to work with her, and I enrolled in one of her two-day seminars. After attending the event, I hired her as my first coach. Caterina taught me things about running my business that I would not have learned in school. It's the stuff you can't just "Google," either. She taught me about sales and marketing (which are totally different to entrepreneurs than in my corporate sales and marketing job), she taught me the importance of leading with my values, she had me experience what being in a supportive community was like, and she stressed the importance of self-care in my business. (Many of these are topics I'm addressing here in this book.) She changed my life forever.

To this day, Caterina is still my coach, and I've hired many other coaches along my journey to help me with different areas of my business. I have a life coach, a few professional speaking coaches, a marketing coach, and a strengths coach. These women help guide me to make decisions that are key to my business growth and success. I will never again be without a coach. There are always areas to uplevel. I loved coaching so much that eventually I was trained as a coach and earned my certification from the International Coach Federation. Coaching is one of the most powerful breakthrough and transformational experiences I've ever had, and I strongly encourage everyone to have a coach. Corporations are catching on to this value, too, as more and more companies are investing in coaches for their leadership teams and staff.

3. Communities

Did your parents ever caution you against running with "the wrong crowd"? Frustrating as it may have been, they had a point. The people you surround yourself with have a powerful impact on your mindset.

Fortunately, you can find fantastic professional and personal communities to support your mindset in mastermind groups, adventure groups, workout teams, or anywhere else you can dream up.

I used to work alone, thinking I could do everything by myself. That was a lonely way of running a business. It wasn't until I met Caterina that I experienced what it would be like to be surrounded by other business owners like me, be in community, and feel 100 percent supported by others. This was a revelation. I experienced new friendships, new ways of thinking, and support beyond what I could imagine. And not only was I getting support, but I was also supporting others in making their business dreams come true. It was a win-win-win.

Being in a professional community can offer many benefits:

- Access to experts who can offer advice and guidance on a wide range of topics
- Networking opportunities with other professionals in your field

- Resources and support for professional development
- Opportunities to learn from others' experiences and mistakes
- A sense of community and belonging to a group of like-minded individuals

Maintaining positivity, showing up the way you want, and going after your goals are all much easier when you're in a community that nurtures your ambitions, your values, and your authentic self. But when you're trying to do it all yourself—or when your network has misaligned values or doesn't understand, believe in, or share your goals—or when others tell you that you must act a certain way, it becomes much more difficult to maintain your ideal mindset.

Surrounding yourself with the right people is essential to your success. From your team to your coaches to your communities, every time you expand your people, you expand your opportunities for growth.

I know firsthand how critical having the right people in our lives and businesses is to our success. 2017 was an extremely difficult year for me. I had left my corporate job to start my business, and five months later my husband was laid off from his job. We went from living on two very healthy corporate incomes to living on the small amount I was making from my start-up consulting firm. We could no longer afford the house we had been in for seventeen years. We had to sell our dream home and move into a tiny rental home. We both were feeling depressed and overwhelmed with the situation. At the same time, my husband was in a car accident and my forty-year-old brother had a heart attack. All of this happened within the span of four months. It was awful.

One day I was looking out the window of the rental home when I saw Tina Shaw, who I had met at a networking event a few years before, walking her Yorkie. I texted Tina to ask if she lived in the neighborhood and, if she did, whether I could start walking my Yorkie with her. She said yes, and we started walking our dogs every morning. After about two weeks of walking together I had an epiphany: I was complaining every single day. Complaining about my situation, about life, about my clients, about everything. I was tired of hearing myself complain. I apologized to Tina about being such a bummer on our walks. I was surprised she even wanted to walk with me.

Tina's response was life changing. She told me about a program called Mastering Life's Energies. It was the first part of the training to become a life coach. She said it was based on "ontology." I had never heard that word before and asked her what that meant. Her reply floored me. She said it was based on how we are "being." I knew immediately I needed to do it. I hated how I was being and was ready to change. I scheduled an appointment with the enrollment counselor and registered to start the next class. I continued beyond the introductory course to complete the entire coach training. Within two years I earned my certification from the International Coach Federation.

Thanks to that serendipitous sighting of Tina and her Yorkie, my two weeks of complaining, and that one conversation about how I was being, my life was forever changed. Tina was the mentor I needed in my life, and the coaching program was the team and community I needed to change my trajectory. The right people showed up, and I took action to connect with them. Since then, I've noticed the right people are always showing up for us, but it's up to us to lean into them.

6

PEOPLE

1. What kind of support do you need to maintain your success mindset?

_____

_____

_____

_____

_____

_____

2. List the top five values you look for in the people you surround yourself with.

_____

_____

_____

_____

_____

_____

_____

3. How would you describe the environment you want to create for your support team?

_____

_____

_____

_____

_____

_____

_____

_____

4. What would it be like if you hired people to do work they love? How would that change your business? How would that change your customers' experience with your business?

_____

_____

_____

_____

_____

_____

_____

5. What kinds of advisors or consultants does your business need? List five people you could reach out to for paid advisory or consulting support, and five people who would make great mentors.

_____

_____

_____

_____

_____

_____

_____

6. Where could you use a coach in your world right now? How would you describe your ideal coach?

_____

_____

_____

_____

_____

_____

_____

7. What kinds of community groups would you benefit from being in? Where can you find out what's available in your community? Identify a business colleague you admire who you could ask what groups they are involved with.

_____

_____

_____

_____

_____

_____

8. What would it be like if you felt 100 percent supported in your business? What difference would it make to you, personally, if you had more support as a leader?

_____

_____

_____

_____

_____

_____

9. Who do you need to let go of that is sucking your energy?

_____

_____

_____

_____

_____

_____

_____

10. Is there a mentor or coaching role you could provide for other leaders to support them? What is the advantage you get from supporting others? What difference would that make in supporting your own vision?

_____

_____

_____

_____

_____

_____

_____

Break the Rules

Following the rules is a good thing, right? When I grew up my parents had rules for me to follow, teachers had rules in classrooms, companies I worked for had rules, and of course I had to follow the rules when driving. Often, these rules are great guideposts and backstops. However, the trouble comes when certain rules no longer serve us. Instead, they inhibit us from being our best. For example, in my corporate job, I was told by one of my managers that I stood out too much, and he instructed me not to talk to the higher-level managers in the company anymore. This left me perplexed; what was I to do when the other managers were around? I had to ignore them because the cost of breaking this rule was likely my job. After months of disliking me, the manager moved me far away from his office, near the back of the sales department I was managing. It felt like a punishment. One might think it was about my performance, but by the two main KPIs—budget and my team's assessment of me as a leader—I was crushing it. Instead, I think his disdain came from his own insecurity about how employees "should" behave toward leadership.

You might be thinking that guy sure was a "Richard." Trust me, I've thought this too! The lesson for me was not about him, however; rather, the message was in how I perceived his feedback and turned his insecurity into a rule that I would practice for a long time to come. The truth is, I'm still practicing it. Any time someone gives me negative feedback, my initial response is to pull back and retreat. But this is no way to be if you're a person on a mission—a person with gifts, knowledge, and inspirational ideas you want to share with the world. (Isn't that who you are, too?)

The rule was that if I stood out, I was bad. That was a rule I needed to break ASAP. Here are some other rules that I followed for far too long:

- **Don't wear pink to speaking engagements.** It's too girly, and you won't be taken seriously. I love pink, but I followed this rule until recently, when I finally squashed it and decided to buy as many pink tops as I could find!
- **Don't cry in business.** It shows how weak you are. I'm not a crier anyway, because someone told me when I was little that I was a crybaby, and that rule stuck. Here's the thing: Crying is a human emotion. Why in the world would we tell people not to cry? It's ok to get mad (if you're a man), but if you cry, you're not good enough.
- **Don't ever take a mental health day.** It means you must be vulnerable. If I had told anyone in the corporate world that I have Generalized Anxiety Disorder, depression, and panic attacks, I probably never would have

gotten the jobs I had, in which I was *always* the top performer. Now that I know how to make space for myself and my mental health, I'm still performing at my peak—and I'm much happier and healthier while doing it.

- **Work whatever hours it takes to get the job done...**even if it's sixty, eighty, or one hundred per a week. The rule I learned here was that there was no time for a life, only business. I ended up burning myself out and getting physically sick (likely the reason for the anxiety and panic, too) until I learned to put boundaries around my work.

My new philosophy is that rules are meant to be broken when they are no longer working for us. People do great things when they shatter the rules. This is where innovation and creativity are born. It doesn't take much research to find great people in history, art, and business who were all rulebreakers. Give yourself some time to really dive deep into your rules and consider what's possible if you, too, become a rulebreaker. In the next journal prompts, I'm going to ask you to identify your rules and start shattering them!

7

RULES

1. What rules have you set for yourself—or believed when someone else set them for you—that are no longer working for you?

_____

_____

_____

_____

2. What are some of the rules you learned in your personal life that have seeped into your business world?

_____

_____

_____

_____

_____

3. How have these rules held you back from having a *Yes!* mindset and creating a *Yes!* environment?

_____

_____

_____

_____

_____

_____

_____

_____

4. How can you start to identify rules in your world that are no longer serving you?

_____

_____

_____

_____

_____

_____

_____

5. Who can support you in creating a list of rules you might be following or demonstrating without even realizing it?

_____

_____

_____

_____

_____

_____

_____

6. What would your life be like if you shattered some of these rules?

_____

_____

_____

_____

_____

_____

_____

7. How could you help tear down rules in your organization that are no longer serving your team?

_____

_____

_____

_____

_____

_____

_____

_____

8. What rules can you start breaking in your industry that would make it a better field for everyone?

_____

_____

_____

_____

_____

_____

_____

_____

9. What are some new rules you would like to set for yourself or your team?

_____

_____

_____

_____

_____

_____

_____

_____

10. How would this help you forge ahead to turn your goals and dreams into reality?

_____

_____

_____

_____

_____

_____

_____

_____

_____

_____

_____

_____

_____

_____

_____

_____

_____

_____

_____

_____

_____

_____

_____

_____

_____

_____

_____

Self-Care

We have all heard that self-care is extremely important. It became very apparent during the pandemic. But who on earth has the time and money to *Eat, Pray, Love* their way through life?

I love to work. I love my business. I feel very accomplished when I am doing a hundred things at once. Strategizing, coaching my clients, speaking to groups, traveling, creating new ideas, and writing this book. It's all fun for me, but there comes a time about every three months when I'm about to crash and burn. My coaches and my team can tell it's coming, and they start encouraging me to take a time-out for self-care. At first, I resisted, because I had always thought of self-care activities as big, expensive things that I didn't have the time or extra money to undertake. Unable to just hop on a plane to a beautiful island for some frosty cocktails, I was frustrated by their requests. But, bless them, my community persisted, and I finally asked them for ideas.

My wonderful colleagues gave me an amazing list of things they do for self-care, and here they are for you to consider adding into your life, too, especially if you (like I did) think you are too busy.

You cannot implement all of these ideas at once, so just circle the ones that are the most appealing to you.

- Walk your dog
- Bike with your kids
- Shut down your computer at 6:30 or 7:00 p.m., and don't look at it again until the next morning
- Don't use your mobile phone at dinner
- Take a five- to seven-minute break and sit in the sun
- Take a ten-minute break and sit under the moon and stars
- Schedule a fifteen-minute break on your calendar and do something besides work
- Sleep until your body wakes naturally (if you can't do this during the week, do it on weekends)
- Schedule a massage, stretching session, salt scrub, or chiropractic appointment
- Read a novel
- Blast your favorite rock song or settle in with your favorite classical composer
- Call a friend or write a letter
- Journal, color with crayons (try breaking the rules and coloring outside the lines), scribble, or doodle
- Meditate, visualize, practice breathing exercises, take a pause
- Take a cardio drumming class
- Play word games, jigsaw puzzles, or bingo

- Cook a healthy meal
- Take a wine and paint class with friends
- Schedule time with a therapist
- Schedule time with a life coach, spiritual coach, or other advisor
- Stand outside when it's raining or snowing and feel the precipitation on your skin
- Make snow angels
- Dance, sing karaoke, sing in the shower or in the car
- Try IV hydration therapy

Most CEOs I work with put their businesses before themselves. Is that you? I was that way myself, but it's a surefire way to burn out. Now, I make time for self-care. It's the first thing on my calendar before I take any appointments. My morning starts with a five-minute snuggle with my dog, followed by a thirty-minute cardio drumming exercise, then a shower. I don't start appointments until 10:30 a.m., and I end them by 4:00 p.m. Some people might think these kinds of boundaries are impossible for them…you have so much work to do, right? What I found was that I was far more productive with this schedule, and I got five times more work done. I was also more happy, creative, and on top of it with my clients instead of burned out, exhausted, and overwhelmed. Self-care is now the most important contributor to my *Yes!* mindset.

Put yourself first, and you AND your business will thrive.

8

SELF-CARE

1. Take a look at the previous list. What new self-care items are you going to add to your life?

_____

_____

_____

_____

_____

_____

2. What can you change about your current situation to make these a priority?

_____

_____

_____

_____

_____

_____

_____

3. Imagine for a minute that you implement one, two, or three new self-care practices into your life. How will that make you feel?

_____

_____

_____

_____

_____

_____

_____

_____

4. How does prioritizing self-care support your business?

_____

_____

_____

_____

_____

_____

_____

5. In what ways can you encourage your team to add self-care into their workdays?

_____

_____

_____

_____

_____

_____

_____

6. What effects would that have on them and your business?

_____

_____

_____

_____

_____

_____

_____

7. How often should you get away from the office for more than four days to get a real break?

---

8. Why is it important to turn off your devices at night or on vacation? Do you do that now? If not, why not? How can you change this behavior? How would that help you to have a *Yes!* mindset?

---

9. Besides your business, what other areas of your life would improve if you implemented more acts of self-care?

_____

_____

_____

_____

_____

_____

_____

10. Name the self-care practice you will commit to right now and declare the date by which you will have implemented it. What will you do to ensure nothing gets in your way?

_____

_____

_____

_____

_____

_____

_____

SAY *Yes* to What You Want

Now that you've equipped yourself with all the tools you need to cultivate and embrace a "Yes" mindset, answer this question for me, right here and now:

What big, life-changing, career-defining idea are you ready to say YES to?

_____

_____

_____

_____

_____

Is this an idea that you're excited about? One that would bring you joy, happiness, and fulfillment to put out into the world?

_____

_____

_____

_____

If so, then I want you to say *yes* to this idea right now. Say it out loud! (Yes, right now, say it!)

There. You've just committed.

Now, go figure it out. You have all the tools you need, including (and most importantly) the mindset that says, "You know what? I *can* do this!"

And the following journal prompts are going to send you on your way.

9

YOUR YES LIST

1. How did it feel to say *yes* to that idea?

_____

_____

_____

_____

_____

_____

2. What are five things you could do *right now* to start making that big idea a reality?

_____

_____

_____

_____

_____

_____

_____

3. What do you need to say "no" to in order to say "yes" to taking action?

_____

_____

_____

_____

_____

_____

_____

_____

4. What things might get in the way of following through on your idea?

_____

_____

_____

_____

_____

_____

_____

5. How can you plan ahead to overcome these fears before they arise?

_____

_____

_____

_____

_____

_____

_____

6. Who can you ask to hold you accountable as you work on your big idea?

_____

_____

_____

_____

_____

_____

_____

_____

7. Write about what you imagine your life will be like when that idea becomes a reality.

_____

_____

_____

_____

_____

_____

_____

_____

_____

_____

_____

_____

_____

_____

_____

_____

_____

The *Yes!* Mindset Ripple Effect

Can the actions you take when you have a *Yes!* mindset change the world? Many people don't believe so, but I do, and I've seen it happen.

Let me share a story with you about one little girl who changed the world for many, and perhaps you'll be convinced that it is possible.

While I was conducting a *Yes!* Attitude workshop, I noticed one of my students was quietly participating and not engaging as much as all the other participants. I wondered if my message meant anything to her. Was she bored to death? Did she think what I was sharing was a load of malarkey? Was she so quiet because she was counting the minutes until it was over?

Three weeks later, I saw her again, and what she had to tell me was amazing! She left the workshop with a deep desire to change the environment around her for her kids. She decided to incorporate one new family project each summer, letting her kids choose the concept. Her ten-year-old daughter, Lira—this beautiful, tiny, olive-skinned, girl with dark hair and big brown eyes—chose to learn how to make balloon animals. Why balloon animals? Lira wanted to deliver them to children in the hospital. That gave Lira's mom an excellent idea. She didn't know how to make balloon animals, but she had another idea that just might bring some cheer to the children's hospital.

Lira's mom had been visiting the farmers' market every week to purchase fresh flowers for her home. She approached her usual flower vendor and asked what happened to the flowers at the end of the day. As she suspected, they were thrown away. She told the vendor her plan, and he agreed to help with the project. Lira visited the vendor at the close of business and got a huge load of flowers. Then she approached the next vendor, and the next, and the next until they had so many flowers they weren't sure what to do.

Lira decided she would go door-to-door and ask the neighbors for jars or old bottles to use for vases. One neighbor gave her several cases of canning jars she wasn't using. Lira now had enough flowers and jars to make nearly fifty bouquets of gorgeous flowers: yellow roses, orange gerbera daisies, purple irises, and white baby's breath. They attached little chalkboard signs to each bouquet, reading, "Have a wonderful day."

Lira, her younger sister Luna, and their mom went to UC Davis Children's Hospital, where they encountered an unexpected obstacle. They learned the children could not receive fresh flowers, because the hospital needed to keep a sterile environment and some kids might have allergies they would want to avoid. It would've been easy to give up and go home disappointed, but Lira, Luna, and their mom summoned a *Yes!* mindset and thought of a new way to spread cheer with their flowers. Lira decided to give the bouquets to all the nurses, doctors, and even the burly security guard, because, she said, "They were special people who took care of the kids." This one little girl had changed the world for fifty others.

But Lira didn't stop there, and she didn't abandon her original idea, either. Within a month, Lira and her mom had learned to make balloon animals, and Lira set up a stand to sell them. She made fifty-three dollars, which she then donated to St Jude's Children's Home. Lira had created a huge ripple effect with her *Yes!* mindset.

You might think this is a personal story, and it is, but it's also a professional story that extended beyond Lira and her mom, beyond the children's hospital workers, and into the business world. Lira's mom went back to work and started telling everyone of her mindset transformation and her adventures. She infected her coworkers, her boss, and her customers with her positive attitude, and soon, the negative water cooler talk had dissipated, transforming into positive stories about kindness. Employee morale went up, communication improved, and there was more team engagement in the office.

Your attitude at work and your attitude at home are connected. When people are in a negative space, it blocks their thought process. They become stuck like a broken record, playing the same negative thoughts over and over while solving nothing. When the negativity is let go and positivity enters the mix, people become more creative and productive. Their job satisfaction increases, and they develop a resilience to negative talk and even to crisis.

It's not always easy to see the silver lining or the bright side in every situation. Even today, Lira's mom calls me to talk about dealing with challenging situations. However, she is aware that mindset is a choice, and she chooses to have an open mind, seek coaching and mentorship, and surround herself with a successful environment. Changing your mindset doesn't happen overnight—it takes hard work. Psychologists suggest it takes three to five positive occurrences to overcome one negative occurrence. But it's worth the effort, because your mindset is powerful and can be a cause of harmony or disarray. **Your mindset is a choice, and you choose every morning how you're going to face the day.**

Lira and her mom put a ripple into the world, and their efforts affected at least fifty people at the hospital, and probably fifty more at Lira's mom's work. My question to you now is, do you believe you can change the world around you? Can you use your *Yes!* mindset to make a difference at home, at work, and in the world? I believe you can, and I challenge you to start today, to make your own ripple effect. Like Lira and her mom, you must be open to the possibilities and take action to make them happen.

RIPPLES

1. Write about a time you were the beneficiary of the mindset ripple effect—when someone else's positive mindset and values-driven leadership inspired you to take action.

_____

_____

_____

_____

_____

2. Write about a time your own mindset led you to do something that started that ripple effect. How did you impact others?

_____

_____

_____

_____

_____

3. What is one action you can take today to start a ripple effect in your business, your industry, or your community?

_____

_____

_____

_____

_____

_____

_____

4. How would it make you feel to start a ripple effect?

_____

_____

_____

_____

_____

_____

_____

_____

5. What would that change about your business and your life?

_____

_____

_____

_____

_____

_____

_____

_____

_____

_____

_____

_____

_____

_____

_____

_____

_____

_____

_____

_____

_____

_____

_____

_____

_____

_____

_____

_____

_____

_____

_____

_____

_____

_____

_____

_____

_____

_____

_____

Ideas for Maintaining Your Mindset

Cultivating and maintaining your *Yes!* mindset isn't a one-and-done activity. Instead, it's a lifelong endeavor that requires care, attention, and perseverance. Awareness of your mindset is the first step to improving. Having a plan of action to take when things start to slip is an ongoing practice to keep you performing at your best. Whenever I get "down in the dumps," I need to have actionable ideas to help me bounce back, because I know that staying in the dumps wreaks havoc on our mental health. I've compiled a list of ideas that have helped me maintain my own mindset over the years, and I encourage you to add your own.

- Watch *A Call to Courage* by Brene Brown, available on Netflix
- Call a friend
- Listen to a TED Talk
- Read *Affirmation Journal for Positive Thinking: Prompts and Inspiration to Help You Harness Peace and Joy* by Kelly Swanson
- Send a handwritten note in the mail
- Pay it forward
- Listen to *The Power of Positive Thinking* by Norman Vincent Peale
- Send flowers to someone you love, just because
- Volunteer for a cause you're passionate about
- Read *Love Yourself Successful* by Katrina Sawa

- Read *Selling with a Servant Heart* by Jim Doyle
- Have tea with a friend
- Make time regularly to review and revise your goals, timelines, and actions
- Watch any episode of *Prides Hollow* by Kelly Swanson on YouTube
- Volunteer for a cause-related event or nonprofit
- Read Jeffrey Gitomer's *Little Gold Book of Yes! Attitude*
- Attend a positive attitude seminar
- Read *Big Magic* by Elizabeth Gilbert
- Call a different relative each month
- Read *You Can Think Differently: Change Your Thinking, Change Your Life* by Caterina Rando
- Read *Mastering Life's Energies* by Maria Nemeth, PhD
- Join a Mastermind Group
- Read *The Little Engine That Could* by Watty Piper
- Buy an adult coloring book and pencils
- Prepare ten "giving bags" for the homeless
- Read *The Science of Getting Rich* by Wallace Wattles
- Donate your used clothes to charity
- Invite your friends to a game night and turn off the phones
- Host a virtual dance party
- Send this book to someone special and share your journal entries with each other

- _____

- _____

- _____

- _____

- _____

The End...or the Beginning

Congratulations! You've made it to the end of this journal. At the risk of sounding cliche, I need to share that this isn't the end; it's the beginning. It's the beginning of a new way of being and a better way of showing up in the world as the leader you were born to be. The stories, strategies and ideas in this book are meant for you to expand on so you can spread your *Yes!* mindset to others. It's meant to spark creativity and innovation to design a way of doing business that is authentic and inclusive. Are you up for the challenge? I think you are! You were born for this!

With every new endeavor, we may experience resistance to change. Remember that this is our brains' way to keep us safe and comfy. I like to think of it as our brains' way of keeping us by a warm fire, reading a book in our pajamas, with a nice cup of hot chocolate with marshmallows. While you should do this sometimes (add it to your list of self-care activities), it is not where we grow. It's not where we make the difference, we came to this world to make. It's in the uncomfortableness of what we are doing that ignites change.

There are three things that will happen when you are entering this new adventure.

1. **Someone is going to tell you that you can't do it**. When I hear this, I like to think my response is "watch me," but the truth is I start to question myself. I worry that I'm not enough, I'm doing it wrong, or it's not normal to always try to see things with a *Yes!* mindset (someone told me that once). When this happens, you must tell yourself that you can do anything you want. Just because someone else doesn't believe it, that doesn't mean you have to. You are on your own journey.

2. **You are going to tell others they can't do that**. This is an interesting way to react to resistance. You start telling others they can't do something, because you don't believe it's possible yourself. We don't do this intentionally or maliciously—it's usually by mistake. It comes out as "that never works for me," or "I tried that before and it didn't work," or "try this way instead." The reality is that what doesn't work for you may work for someone else, because they are on their own journey. Be mindful of turning your own limiting beliefs into resistance for others.

3. **You are going to tell yourself that you can't do that**. This is the most likely thing to happen. Some of the things I've told myself are that I don't have the time to focus on this, it's too hard, and I don't have what I need. Another set of

things I say to myself are that I can't do this because of outside forces holding me back, like other people, the weather, the economy, the pandemic. All these reasons sound legit, and it would be easy to accept them as my reality. The truth is, though, I have done the most amazing work during what others have defined as the most challenging times, and so can you. I mean who becomes a cardio drumming fitness instructor at the age of fifty after having been a couch potato?

You are now fully aware of the resistance you'll face, which means you cannot ignore it. Do yourself a favor and embrace it for what it is…baseless negativity. *You* are doing the work, and you are making the changes you want to see in your business and life. Celebrate the uncomfortable place you are in, because it means you are entering new territory.

Have fun and enjoy the adventure!

Acknowledgements

Thank you to my friend and mentor Kevin O'Brien, who first supported me to put my dream of sharing my messages of positivity into the world. I'm forever grateful for the special way you contributed to this book.

To my husband, Steve, who always tells me that I am meant to share positive messages with the world. When I often question whether I'm good enough, you remind me that I was born for this. Thank you, I could not put myself out there like this without your wind at my sails.

To my immediate team, Carrie, Teresa, Marilyn: you are more than business colleagues, you are family. I couldn't do all of this without you. To my incredible editor, Sarah, thank you for adding your brilliance to this book; you are a very gifted editor. To my clients, I learn every day from being your coach and consultant. I'm blessed to be your partner.

To my coaches, Caterina, Katrina, Elizabeth, Jane, Lois, Michelle and Kelly, thank you for not letting me get in my own way and challenging me to shatter the rules!

To Maria and the coaches at the Academy of Coaching Excellence, thank you for giving me the tools to look, see, tell the truth, and take authentic action.

To the great Jeffrey Gitomer, you have been my longest-time coach, and it was you who sparked my interest in becoming a lifelong student of positive attitude. Your *Little Gold Book of Yes! Attitude* and your generosity in allowing me to facilitate the *Yes! Attitude* workshop changed my life.

To all my students and readers, thank you for showing up for yourselves and taking the plunge into this book. You are right where you are meant to be, and I'm cheering you on every step of the way!

About the Author

Think "force of nature" in the best possible way. Jennifer Darling has been working with business owners for over twenty-five years and has a knack for successfully leading businesses and teams through turbulent times.

Jennifer has a master's degree in management with an emphasis in change, and she is an International Coaching Federation certified coach and lifelong student of positive mindset and attitude. Jennifer spent many of her professional years in advertising sales and sales management for media giants Hearst Television and Comcast. She had some of her most successful times while navigating the 2007-2009 recession and the 2020 pandemic. She knows what it takes to have a *Yes!* mindset even when things seem to be out of your control.

For nearly a decade, Jennifer has owned her own coaching, consulting, and speaking practice where she teaches people how to engage innovatively, connect more effectively, and increase their visibility in new and valuable ways. Her powerful messages encourage leaders to embrace change and show up authentically. She delivers keynotes, seminars, workshops, and virtual trainings on leadership, sales and marketing, change, and mindset.

Jennifer is the author of the wildly popular books *Say Yes! (Then Figure It Out)*, *Find Your Leadership Rhythm*, *Increase Your Leads with LinkedIn: 52 Tips for Sales Success* and *Discover Your Inspiration.*

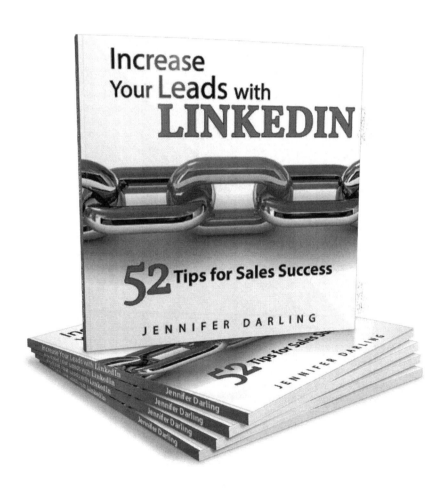

OTHER TITLES FROM JENNIFER DARLING

JENNIFER'S SPEECH TOPICS

Say Yes! Then Figure It Out

- Harness the power of a Yes! Mindset for greater influence and impact within your team, business, and industry.
- Unleash your inner rockstar through bold, innovative moves to seize opportunities and reach the next level of success!
- Design a Yes! Environment to foster a culture of collaboration, innovation, creativity and learning.

Find Your Leadership Rhythm

- **R**hythm: Amp Up Your Volume and Visibility
- **O**pportunity: Try New Things and Write New Tracks
- **C**adence: Get Your Team Drumming to the Same Beat
- **K**it: Create a Success Environment Where You're Ready to ROCK

Rock Your Sales Results

....

Key Takeaways:

- Create More Opportunities with Lead Generators that Attract Today's Buyers
- Position Yourself as the Go-To-Expert with People Who Are Ready to Buy
- Reset Your Mindset for Results Beyond Your Imagination

Increase Your Sales Leads on LinkedIn

....

Key Takeaways:

- Establish Yourself as the Go-To Expert
- Create More Opportunities for Business with a Wide and Deep Network
- Build Top-of-Mind Awareness so Prospects Think of You First
- Attract Ideal Customers Ready to Buy with a Stand-Out Profile

Expand Your Leadership Presence on LinkedIn

Key Takeaways:

- Build your professional brand and position yourself LinkedIn
- Create an outstanding profile to command the attention of your stakeholders
- Increase your network of influential connections

CONNECT WITH JENNIFER

Email: Jennifer@JenniferDarlingSpeaks

Website: *JenniferDarlingSpeaks*

LinkedIn.com/in/JenniferDarlingSpeaks

Facebook.com/DarlingCoaching

Twitter.com/TheRealJDarling

YouTube.com/c/JenniferDarlingSalesExpert

BOOK Jennifer to Speak
for your Next Event: